Make Your Own
JEWISH CALENDAR
Coloring Book

Chaya Burstein

DOVER PUBLICATIONS, INC.
New York

Bibliographical Note

Make Your Own Jewish Calendar Coloring Book is a new work, first published by Dover Publications, Inc., in 1995.

International Standard Book Number: 0-486-28630-4

Manufactured in the United States of America
Dover Publications, Inc., 31 East 2nd Street, Mineola, N.Y. 11501

Jewish Holidays and the Jewish Calendar

The Jewish calendar is lunisolar—that is, it follows the solar year, but the months are determined by the cycle of the moon. As the calendar exists today, it probably dates from as late as the fourth century CE (Common Era). Because the arrangement of months runs approximately 11 days beyond the solar year, an extra month (Second Adar) is added to seven out of the 19 years in a repeating 19-year cycle.

This may seem complicated, but if you follow the instructions that follow, you can create your own calendar for the Jewish year, including in it all the important dates and festivals.

Following a standard practice, we are basing our calendar on the calendar in day-to-day use, the European or Gregorian calendar. Begin by making the Gregorian calendar. All you have to do is write in the number for each day on the monthly squares. Start with the first day of the year, January 1. Once you have found the correct day of the week for January 1 in the year you want, number the rest of the month. January has 31 days. When you complete January, begin numbering February, which has 28 days, except during leap years (1996, 2000 and every four years after that), when it has 29. March, May, July, August, October and December all have 31 days; all the other months (April, June, September and November) have 30. There are 365 days in a year, except in a leap year, which has 366.

If a month with 30 days begins on a Saturday, write two dates (23 and 30) on the last Sunday box. If a month with 31 days begins on a Friday, write two dates (24 and 31) in the last Sunday box. If a 31-day month begins on a Saturday, write 23 and 30 in the last Sunday box and 24 and 31 in the last Monday box.

The list that follows gives the Jewish months of the year (in their own sequence), the *approximate* Gregorian months in which they fall, and any important date that occurs within them. Dates of holidays can vary widely from year to year. In 1994, for example, Hanukkah began November 28, but in 1995 it is scheduled for December 18. Sometimes the date of a holiday is changed to avoid having it fall on the Sabbath. Local religious institutions will have calendars indicating the days on which the holidays fall in the year for which you are making your calendar. Copy them onto this calendar, and you will be ready to celebrate the cycle of the Jewish year. (Remember, a holiday begins at sunset the day preceding the date by which it is listed on the calendar.)

If you wish, you can also enter the names and days of the Jewish months in the boxes by referring to the same religious calendar.

Tishri (*September/October*). **1 & 2:** Rosh Ha-Shanah, the New Year, is ushered in by blowing the *shofar* (ram's horn) in the synagogue. Sweets, including apples dipped in honey, are eaten to start the year with sweetness. Rosh Ha-Shanah marks the beginning of the High Holy Days, the Ten days of Penitence. **10:** Yom Kippur, the Day of

Atonement, the most solemn day in the Jewish year, is observed by fasting and prayers for forgiveness for sins committed during the year. **15–22:** Sukkot, the Feast of Tabernacles. A harvest festival, it is celebrated by taking meals in a *sukkah*, a booth constructed under the sky that is covered with leaves, branches and harvest fruits. **23:** Simhat Torah (joy in the Torah), marks the reading of the last chapter of the Torah in the synagogue. (The reading of the Torah, in weekly chapters, takes the full year.)

Heshvan *(October/November).*

Kislev *(November/December).* **25:** The first day of the eight days of Hanukkah, the Festival of Lights. The holiday recalls the rededication of the Temple in Jerusalem after Judah Maccabee drove foreigners out of Israel. The Temple was cleansed, but only a little oil was available to burn in the *menorah,* or candelabrum. By a miracle, the oil lasted eight days. This is commemorated by lighting the candles of the *menorah* at sundown for eight days. Hanukkah is a joyous time, when families have festive meals, play with the *dreidel* (top) and give presents to children. *Latkes* (potato pancakes) are a special holiday delicacy.

Tevet *(December/January).* **2:** The end of Hanukkah.

Shevat *(January/February).* **15:** Tu Bi-Shevat, the New Year of Trees. In Israel, trees are planted. In northern climates, where winter planting is not possible, nuts, dates, figs and raisins from Israel are eaten.

Adar *(February/March).* **14:** Purim, the Feast of Lots. The Book of Esther is read in the synagogue. It tells the story of how Queen Esther, wife of the King of Persia, was able to foil the evil Haman in his plot to destroy the Jews. Members of the congregation stamp their feet and twirl *groggers* (noisemakers) to drown out the name of Haman whenever it is read. Children parade in costumes. A special pastry eaten during the festival is the *hamantash,* a triangular confection usually filled with prunes or poppy seeds.

Second Adar. This is the extra, "leap-year" month mentioned above.

Nisan *(March/April).* **15–22:** Passover (Pesach) memorializes the delivery of the Jewish people from slavery in Egypt about 3500 years ago. A special meal, the *seder,* is served, at which various dishes symbolizing slavery and freedom are eaten. The Haggadah, telling the story of Passover, is read, and the youngest child of the household poses four questions relating to the holiday. Leavened bread cannot be eaten during Passover; *matzo,* a flat, hard bread, is eaten instead.

Iyyar *(April/May).* **5:** Israeli Independence Day. The state was proclaimed on May 14, 1945. **18:** Lag Ba-Omer celebrates the life of Shimon Bar Yohani, who taught the Torah despite a ban imposed by the Romans. Today students observe it with outside activities such as picnics and sports competitions.

Sivan *(May/June).* **6 & 7:** Shavuot, a spring harvest festival, also celebrates the Lord's gift of the Torah and the Ten Commandments to the Jewish people. Flowers and leafy branches decorate the synagogue, and such dairy foods as noodle pudding and *blintzes* (crepes) are eaten.

Tammuz *(June/July).*

Av *(July/August).* **9:** Tisha Be-Av commemorates the destruction of the First and Second Temples and the Exile of the Jews. It is a day of mourning and fasting.

Elul *(August/September).*

In addition to the holidays they show, the illustrations in the calendar also depict the following aspects of Jewish life:

January: At sunset on Friday, a family ushers in the Sabbath, the seventh day of the week, which was set aside by the Lord as a day of rest after the six days of Creation. The mother of the family lights and blesses the Sabbath candles. *Hallah,* a braided bread, lies under an embroidered cover on the table.

November. The illustration shows various religious objects. LEFT, TOP: A seven-branched *menorah.* LEFT, BOTTOM: A *kippah,* or head cap worn in synagogue, and *tefillin* or phylacteries, boxes containing written prayers, are strapped on by male worshippers during weekday prayer services. CENTER: The Torah, the five books of Moses, written on parchment by scribes. RIGHT, TOP: Ner Tamid, the eternal light, that burns continually in front of the ark in which the Torah is kept. Below are the *shofar;* the *mezuzah,* containing a prayer, which is fixed on the doorways to Jewish homes; and a *tallit,* or fringed prayer shawl.

SABBATH

JANUARY

Sunday	Monday	Tuesday	Wednesday	Thursday	Friday	Saturday

Tu Bi-Shevat

FEBRUARY

Sunday	Monday	Tuesday	Wednesday	Thursday	Friday	Saturday

PURIM

MARCH

Sunday	Monday	Tuesday	Wednesday	Thursday	Friday	Saturday

APRIL

Sunday	Monday	Tuesday	Wednesday	Thursday	Friday	Saturday

Israeli Independence Day

MAY

Sunday	Monday	Tuesday	Wednesday	Thursday	Friday	Saturday

SHAVUOT

JUNE

Sunday	Monday	Tuesday	Wednesday	Thursday	Friday	Saturday

Tisha Be-Av

JULY

Sunday	Monday	Tuesday	Wednesday	Thursday	Friday	Saturday

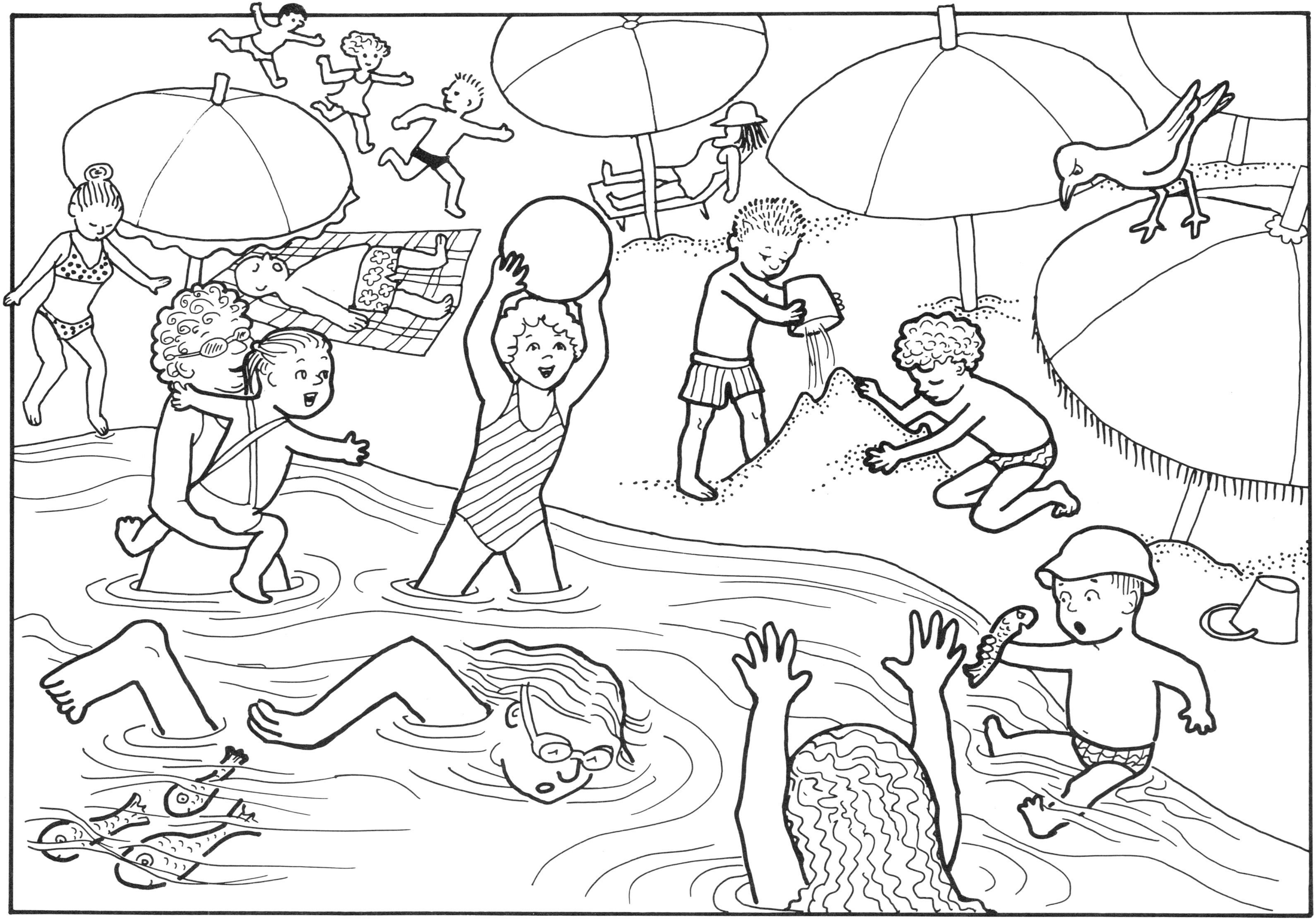

Vacation

AUGUST

Sunday	Monday	Tuesday	Wednesday	Thursday	Friday	Saturday

Rosh Ha-Shanah

SEPTEMBER

Sunday	Monday	Tuesday	Wednesday	Thursday	Friday	Saturday

OCTOBER

Sunday	Monday	Tuesday	Wednesday	Thursday	Friday	Saturday

JEWISH RELIGIOUS OBJECTS

NOVEMBER

Sunday	Monday	Tuesday	Wednesday	Thursday	Friday	Saturday

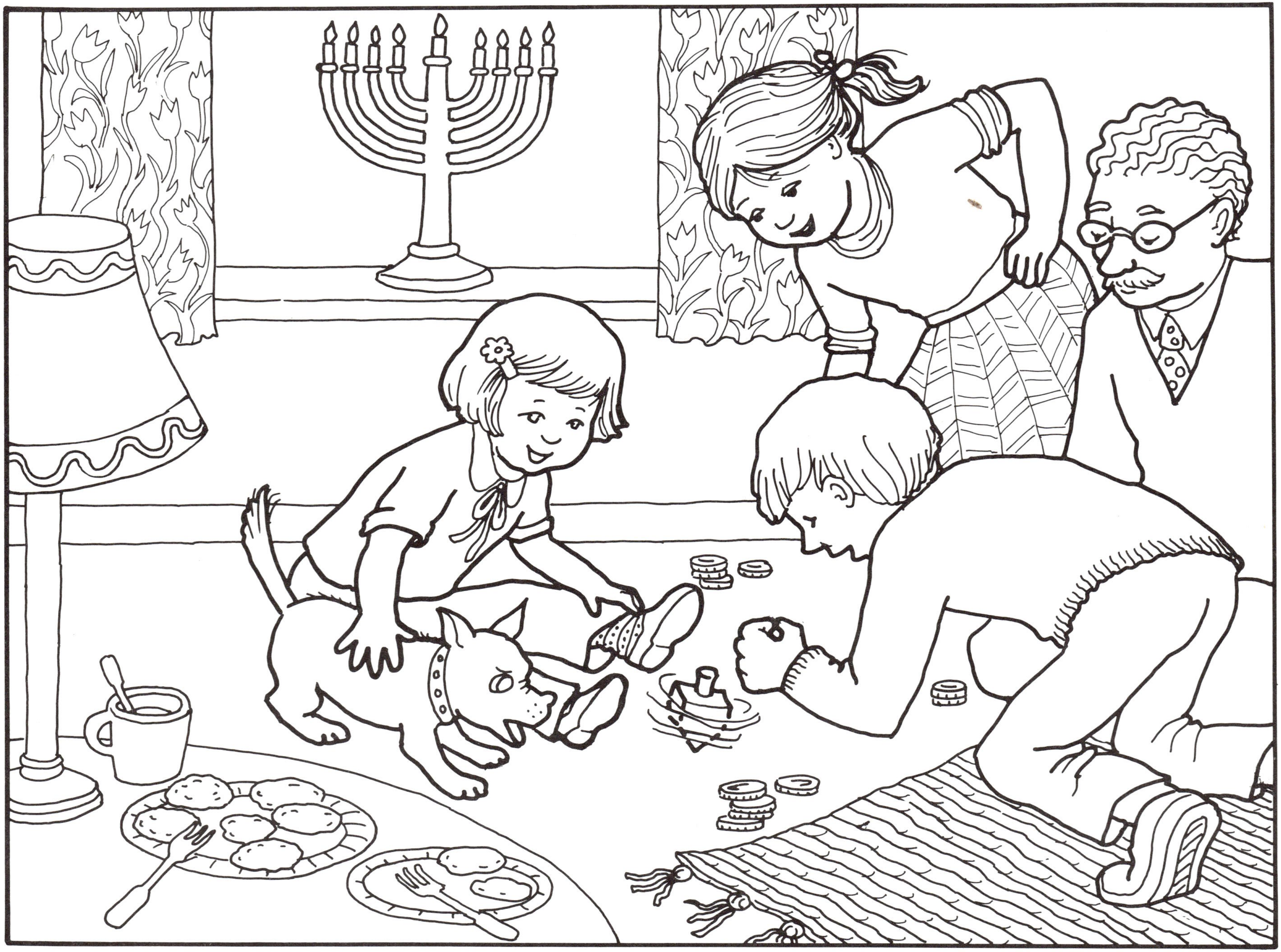

Hanukkah

DECEMBER

Sunday	Monday	Tuesday	Wednesday	Thursday	Friday	Saturday